Introduction

For me the best part of being a home based entrepreneur and investor is the freedom.

Freedom to work the hours I chose instead of being tied to a job and working specific hours dictated by a boss. Freedom to take tea breaks and lunch breaks when I want to take them and for whatever duration of time I chose the breaks to be. I can meet a friend and have two or three hours for lunch if I chose to. Freedom to take holidays when I want to instead of being given 3 weeks holidays at my boss' discretion. I enjoy the freedom of no longer commuting to and from work. I have total freedom.

These days I work when I chose to work. I'm an early riser and I like to take advantage of that. This morning, I woke up at 4:30am and still in my dressing gown, I did four hours work before the rest of the family woke up. I've already done more work by 8:30am than most people get done in a full day. You might not like the idea of getting up at 4:30am but prefer to work a few hours while the kids are in school or late in the evening once they've gone to bed. Working from home gives you the freedom to work the hours that suit you.

When my 14 year old daughter is on school holidays so am I. That works out at around 175 days a year of holidays. To put it into perspective it is almost 6 months of holidays a year as opposed to the 3 weeks of holidays I would be allowed to take if I was an employee. I don't have to worry about expensive child minding services when school is shut. I am able to spend as much time as possible with my daughter. Hopefully, she realises how much she benefits from having mum around a more than if I had a traditional job.

My businesses and my investments can be run from anywhere in the world. All I need is a laptop, internet connection and a mobile phone. Officially, I have an office at home but if I choose to sit on the beach when the sun shines then the beach becomes my office for the hour or two that I may spend working. By having a mobile office I am able to go skiing for weeks at a time, do an hour or so work each morning before the ski field opens and then I can enjoy the rest of the day skiing. My businesses and investments keep making money whether I choose to work or not.

I have the type of lifestyle many can only dream about and the wealth to enjoy it. But it hasn't always been that way. The secret to creating this kind of lifestyle is having multiple streams of income. That is income which comes from having businesses and investments that require little management time, no staff and are cash rich.

Starting your own business doesn't mean working all hours of the night and day. Granted, it may take some initial effort to get the business up and running but in the longer term running your own business should be about providing you with the freedom to do what you want to do when you want to do it and having the money to do it.

If you are tied to a business that takes up 10- 15 hours a day, 7 days a week you haven't built a business you have created a job. Building a business is about working on your business not in your business. Throughout this book you will find ways to create free time. Take advantage of it and enjoy it. Isn't that why you started your business in the first place?

Niche marketing is the perfect business for creating income and free time. Most of the work can be subcontracted to a fulfilment company reducing the time spent working in the business allowing you more time to work on the business. Once your system is in place it can continue creating income for a long time.

Do you want more freedom?

Do you want a better lifestyle?

Do you want more wealth?

Would you prefer to work from home at hours to suit you?

Do you want a business with low overheads?

Do you want a business with high profit and income?

If you answered 'YES' to any of the above questions then this book is probably what you've been looking for.

Table of Contents

Surviving 2013

Make A Living From Property

Beginners Guide to the Sharemarket

Other Books by Karen

Legal

The right of Karen Newton to be identified as Author has been asserted in accordance with the Copyright, Designs and Patent Act 1988

Section 1

Starting Your Own Business

Section 1 - Introduction

When I look at the businesses I have or have had over the past 24 years that I have been an entrepreneur they all have one thing in common. They were all based on activities or interests that I or my husband had at the time.

The first business was set up in 1989. It was a specialist welding company aimed at the vintage and veteran car market. It expanded to become a business dealing in specialist repairs for insurance companies.

My husband, who is crazy about cars and motor racing, was at the time involved in racing go karts and competing in hill climbs and rallying. He frequently needed repairs on his racing vehicles and would complain about being unable to find a business to do the work he needed. Fed up with the problem he went to night classes learnt a trade as a welder and specialist welding.

At the night classes he found people with vintage and veteran cars also learning how to weld specialist metals. He came up with the idea of setting up a specialist welding business and together with a friend 'Fusiontech' was started.

As both partners were involved with various clubs they advertised their services through the clubs and soon had a successful little business. Eventually, they were approached by some insurance repair companies to provide quotes for more difficult welding jobs and the business grew.

By looking at problems around him and finding ways to solve the problem, my husband built his first business.

Richard Branson is one of the UK's best known entrepreneurs. He owns the Virgin brand and has over 300 companies operating under the Virgin name. Richard Branson sees a problem and sets up a company to solve it. Virgin Airlines was started when Richard was stuck in America. Airlines are notorious for double booking seats. Richard was the unfortunate recipient of being bumped off a flight. Stuck in America he chartered an aeroplane and offered one way tickets at a discount price to fill the plane and Virgin Airlines was born. His companies are successful because he solves other people's problems. The more people you can help with their problems the more successful you become.

Deirdre Bounds is a stand-up comic who set up a business from her bedsit. The business called i-to-i became one of the biggest gap year companies. Deirdre sold it to a FTSE100 company, Tui Travel, for an eight figure sum. In other words, Deirdre solved a problem for gap year students who wanted to work and travel overseas. The more students she helped the bigger her business became. The more problems she solved the wealthier she became.

Emma Sinclair is a woman I met earlier this year. She worked in Investment Banking and decided to leave because the long hours were not favourable for a family life. Emma was working from home when her ex-bosses asked her to do some overseas work for them. This grew to more and more customers and within a very short time listed her home based business on the stock market. Emma became the youngest person ever to list a share market company. Emma's business provided services to international organisations and customers and in doing so created a company that could be list on the share market and substantial wealth.

For me my businesses also involve solving problems for other people. One of my businesses is lending money to individuals and companies who are struggling to find finance due to banks reducing the amount they will lend to the public. I lend to them through P2P and Angel Investing. This business is successful because a lot of people have been affected by the banks failure to lend. Through the lending business I solve a lot of problems for a lot of people. In return I have a successful business.

Another business is niche marketing. People need and want information about specific topics. By providing that information in the format of books, ebooks, newsletters, dvd and downloads I solve a problem for many people and in return I have a successful business.

The more problems you can find and offer possible solutions to the more people you can help the more successful your business becomes.

So, what problems do you have?

What solutions can you come up with to solve those problems?

How many business ideas do you have?

A couple of years ago, my family and I were having diner at a restaurant with some friends who run their own business. My daughter, who was only 12 at the time, told our friends she was thinking about running her own business. 'What do you want to do?' asked our friend. Our daughter started telling him all the ideas she had. At their encouragement she wrote on a napkin a list of businesses she wanted to build. Our daughter put the list together by thinking about all the problems she sees around her and how she would go about trying to put them right. The list consists of 15 business opportunities and around 12 of them have the potential to become very successful enterprises.

If you can't come up with any problems that need sorting try asking members of your family or friends. Then ask your children or friends kids to come up with some answers on how to solve the problem. Children are very creative and I'm sure they will easily come up with some business ideas for you.

Most successful businesses find a problem to solve. The more people you can solve the problem for the more successful business you will have.

So what are you waiting for? Go and find some problems to solve.

Working on Your Business not In Your Business

Many people start a business because they are fed up with working in their current job. They don't like the boss. They don't like the hours. They want to have holidays when they decide to take them not when they are told to take them. Some people start in business because they have been made redundant. They know the business or industry well and feel they could do a better job and probably at a cheaper rate if they run their own business.

They set up a business and before long have a good customer base, because they are cheaper than their ex employer. The business grows and they find themselves working longer hours to fit in all the customer jobs. The administration work of invoicing customers, paying the bills, filing tax returns are pushed into the background and only done out of urgency. Soon the business owner is working 10 – 15 hours a day and getting into a rut of non-stop work. The very reason they left their employment in the first place was to avoid these kind of working conditions. Only now, instead of working 8 hours a day they are working 15 hours a day. Instead of having three weeks holidays a year they are working fifty two weeks a year. Instead of a better quality of life it is worse as they no longer have time to spend with their family. Instead of healthily growing their business they are panicking because if they don't work they will lose a customer(s) and then there will be less money coming in. They are in a never ending cycle and the business is in real trouble.

What did they do wrong? The answer is simple. They worked in their business not on their business.

Working on your business is a strange concept to many would be business owners and is one of the reason 80% of business fail in the first five years of trading. As a business owner your responsibility is to your business. You have to think of your business as a separate entity and what you are going to do to help that entity succeed.

As a business owner you need to be able to take a detached look at your business and assess what the needs of the business are. What do you want to achieve with this business and how do you intend to go about doing that? What areas of the business need improving to help you meet your goals for the business? If you are spending all your time working in your business how can you take the time to put your business plans in place; your marketing plans; your customer plans; your infrastructure plans; how can you keep an eye on what competitors are doing? All the things you need to know to run your business successfully.

One of my first business mentors, a gentleman named Vince, said he took two weeks holidays every seven weeks. For the first week he would just be winding down relaxing. The second week he would be developing ideas for the business. On returning to work he would start implementing the changes. After seven weeks of changes and monitoring the effects he would take another two weeks off work and the whole process would start again.

Vince had learned the hard way. He had two businesses, a bakery and a florist. With the bakery he would start at two o'clock in the morning preparing his bread mix, allowing the yeast to work, start baking so he had fresh break ready to sell when he opened his shop at 6am. He closed at 12:00 and went to his florist shop where he made his orders and deliveries and spent the evening ringing international orders through the various countries. He would clean his shops, do paperwork and find he only had time for a few hours sleep so he slept in the bakery ready to start work again at 2:00am. His health deteriorated and so did his family life. He found he was making very little money and the family were struggling to make ends meet. He decided there had to be a different way.

The first thing he did was take a couple of days off work and look at how he could improve the business. He realised he spent too much time working in the business and not enough time working on the business. He came up with a plan and implemented it. Part of the plan was to have a holiday every seven weeks. It didn't happen over night but it did happen. Both the bakery and the florist became franchises. He set up other businesses that also became franchises. He now has a dream lifestyle, houses around the world, private jet and luxury cars and still takes his holidays every seven weeks. He works on his businesses not in his businesses.

A few months ago, my daughter and I, were both at a beauty therapist and my daughter started asking the therapist how easy or difficult the beauty business was to run. How much stock she held and the customer basis? The beauty therapist's response was 'are you thinking of studying to become a beauty therapist when you leave school?' 'No,' replied my daughter 'I'm not going to work in it. I'm going to employ the people I need to do that'. I was so proud of her and her understanding of business. At the age of 13 my daughter has already taken her first steps to building her business empire by working <u>on</u> her business not <u>in</u> her business.

Remember, it is easier to set a business up the right way from the start rather than to get yourself so involved in the day to day operations of the business that you then have difficulty replacing yourself in the business preventing you from working on the business rather than in it.

Which Business Structure Should You Use?

Note: This book is written for the UK. There are different laws and regulations in other countries and you should seek the advice of a person suitably qualified in your country to advise you on starting a new business.

Far too many people get stuck on business structure before they even have a business up and running. Questions such as, 'should I form a limited company?' seem more important than 'who are my customers? What do they want? And what products do I need to sell them?'

My advice is to start trading and only form a Limited Company when your accountant advises you to do so. It can be costly and time consuming to set up a company and then find your business fails. You will have wasted a lot of money. Start as a sole trader and if you don't like the business or it is not successful it is easier to close down. However, you shouldn't go into business with the attitude that it will fail because inevitably it will fail.

Once your business is growing nicely your accountant will advise you on the best structure for your business and when you should be changing the status of the business. Normally, structural change is for tax purposes or to protect you legally or when you start employing staff or subcontracting the work.

Your initial job should be to find customers and sell your product – no customer, no business.

However, if you intend to go into business with a friend, an acquaintance or even a family member you need to have a formal structure in place detailing who will be doing what. Who is going to be responsible for sales and marketing of the business; who will be responsible for the day to day activities; who will be paid what. A limited partnership may be better than setting up a company.

Working with a friend or family member puts strain on the relationship and many friendships and marriages have broken down as a consequence. Drawing up a legal agreement between you before you start the business will save a lot of headaches in the future. Having said that my business partner for over 23 years has been my husband we work well together and compliment each others strengths and weaknesses. So don't rule out your spouse as a business partner.

Business Plan

Businesses don't plan to fail, they fail to plan.

A business plan doesn't need to be elaborate. It can be written down on a single piece of paper. But having a plan is essential otherwise it is too easy to become side tracked and before you know it your business is in a terminal state.

My Business Plan

For a new business I have a very simple business plan format:

1. What do I want to achieve with this business – does this business have the potential to be a large business, will it remain as a small business, is it suitable for a franchise.
2. Who are my customers likely to be – is my product or service aimed at teenagers, women, men or everyone. Which country will it be in? Will it be the UK, Europe or Worldwide.
3. How am I going to let my potential customers know about the business – is it going to be word of mouth, advertising on television, newspaper advertising, online advertising or direct mailing advertising.
4. What will I need immediately to start this business – will I need a telephone line for orders to be rung through or will a mobile be suitable, will I process online orders so do I need a computer or do I already have one. Can I use a fulfilment centre or will I be doing the work myself. Do I need stock or can I use a drop ship company. If I'm holding stock what minimum do I have to buy and

where will I store it. Do I need to manufacture the product and if so what machinery will I need. Where will I be located? Can I run it from home or do I need premises.

5. How much time do I need to dedicate to this? Will one hour a day be enough to get it up and running or is it going to be eight hours a day.

6. What timeframe am I allowing to build this business? Will I need six months a year or will I know in 6 weeks if it is going to work or not.

7. What training will I need? Will I need some marketing, selling and business management skills? Where do I get this information from?

8. And finally, how much is all this going to cost?

Don't skimp on planning your business. There is a saying 'marry in haste, repent at leisure'. It can be equally applied to business. Rush to set up a business and if the planning isn't in place the business will likely fail. If your budgets are completed how will you know how much capital you need to start the business? How much cashflow do you need to run your business effectively until the business is making a profit? Many successful businesses have failed not because they were bad businesses but because they had insufficient cashflow or capital to get them through the difficult times. No matter how good your business is every business will go through a bad patch. Make it part of your business plan to consider how you will deal with this situation when it arises.

Consider how quickly you want the business to grow. We all think it would be fantastic if a business grows quickly but if it is too quickly how will you fund the growth and what staff will you need to cope with the growth.

A friend of mine runs a manufacturing business. He developed a product which he advertised on the QVC shopping channel. He was advised he could expect to sell about 10,000 items. He thought this was good and achievable within his business model. He could cope with that quantity fulfil the orders and once done would be ready to advertise again.

He planned to advertise twice a year on QVC. His business could cope with 20,000 items a year. He had other core manufacturing business. The 20,000 items could be fitted around the other work on existing machinery. As the profit came in from the sales he would invest the money into new machinery and staff allowing him to increase production. The following year he should be able to increase his advertising and production to around 75,000 items a year.

His product was advertised on QVC shopping channel and immediately he had 1 million orders. Now he had a big problem. He had insufficient capital to buy machinery capable of handling the quantity of production to meet the orders. The machinery he needed was in China and would take around 3 months to be shipped out to him. He had to take on more staff and train them to use the machinery. In the meantime he had to fulfil normal manufacturing orders.

To cut a long story short he managed to complete the orders with assistance from his wife, three sons and daughter in laws working 7 days a week 20 hours a day for a few months.

Planning can't always be perfect but good planning should enable a business to get over any difficulties and develop to the next stage. Make controlled growth part of your business plan.

Making A Decision

Once I have the business plan in place I then put it aside for a few days and think really hard about whether or not this is the best business I can set up at this very moment.

I have a folder of business plans and ideas. On a regular basis I review the folder and decide if it is the right time to start this business? Sometimes you can have a really good idea but the timing is wrong or I can't source the right supplier or products at this very moment. Instead of throwing the idea away I file it for a future review.

Just because I have made the decision not to proceed with the business at this moment in time it doesn't mean the business won't work at another time or in another location. Unless it is an absolutely ludicrous idea there is always a right time and right location to start any business. You just have to find it.

Let's say I've decided to open a business which will supply ski assistance facilities for disabled people. My current location is an absolute waste of time as the mountain near me rarely gets any snow. I would be lucky if it gets a week of snow in winter and then it isn't deep enough to ski on. However, I have an apartment in the French Alps where you can normally ski for around seven months of the year from October to May. The best location for this business is obviously France. Unfortunately, timing is not good because I spend 11 months of the year in Britain. Starting up a business and running it in France would be difficult.

However, if I were supplying information on how to set up a ski assistance facility business for disabled people I could run an information business from anywhere in the world. A different slant on a business idea can make a big difference between it becoming a viable business idea or not.

I have a property management business which I set up to manage my property portfolio. I did very little with it, in fact, the company was dormant for years. By chance, I met a couple earlier this year with whom I have built a working relationship. They seem the perfect couple to run a property management business. The dormant business idea is now a thriving franchise business. One idea to manage my property became a franchise to manage property for many landlords. Not only was the initial timing wrong for the business but so was the business structure. By being patient and waiting for the right timing and then putting the right structure and systems in place a dormant business is now a thriving business.

Take a look at your list of business ideas and see which are possible to set up now, which need to be filed for future reference. How many different ways could these businesses be run?

Bank Accounts

One thing you will need to start trading is a bank account. Most banks offer business accounts with a fee free period usually around 12 to 18 months to give you time to get your business up and running and making some cash. Shop around and see which bank will offer you the best deal.

Cheque Account – you will need a checking account so you can pay for any expenses as they arise. Although some companies do still accept payment by cheque these days most companies prefer payments to be made through internet banking and/or debit cards.

Savings Account is not necessary but I do recommend having one. Once your business is trading and you have cash going into your account put some of it into a savings account to pay your taxes. There is nothing worse than having your tax bill and wondering where you are going to get the money to pay it. Many businesses have been closed down due to being unable to pay the tax bill. If you get into the habit of putting a certain percentage away each month then you should not have any worries about taxes.

Credit/Debit Card Facilities – unless you are opening a retail outlet and need to let your customers pay with a debit or credit card I would not worry about this facility. If you are accepting payments online then paypal or other providers are your best option. You can accept payment by debit or credit card and pay only as you use the service. If you take a bank facility you will be paying every month whether you make money or not.

In today's modern technology world most people have a smartphone. There are several organisations that allow you to use your smartphone to accept credit/debit card facilities. Barclays have the pingit system and you don't have to bank with them to use it you only have to register your mobile with them.

Taxes

When you start in business you have 90 days to inform Inland Revenue that you have started a business. There are some hefty penalties if you fail to do so.

You are required to pay NIC contributions immediately but Inland Revenue will give you an exemption if your expectations for the first year sales are low. But you still need to register with Inland Revenue and send in the exemption request within 90 days of starting your business.

- For more information visit www.**hmrc**.gov.uk/**businesses/**iwt**register**-a-new-**business**.shtml

Tax Returns will need to be completed on an annual basis. An accountant and/or tax advisor is the best person for completing and filing the return on your behalf. They have knowledge and expertise on what can or can't be claimed as a tax deduction. Don't be tempted to try and file the returns yourself just to save money. In the long run an accountant and/or tax advisor will save you a lot of money and stress.

Which Accountant Should You Use?

I started in business 24 years ago. Since that time I have used a number of accountants. Some are good and some are bad. My recommendation is to interview accountants until you get the right one for you and your business.

When interviewing the accountants you are looking for someone who has experience and knowledge in the industry you want to work in.

When I started with property rentals I interviewed several accountants before deciding on the one I use today. The reason I chose him was because
1. He offered free advice on starting my business
2. He made the process of providing information very simple
3. He had other clients who had large thriving property investment businesses.
4. He didn't object to being interviewed. Many accountants were clearly irritated when asked for an interview and some refused.

If you build up the relationship with the accountant as you build your business then his advice will be extremely useful as your business grows. If you are starting a residential property investment business an accountant will advise you from the outset about tax relief and the best way forward. There are some tax allowances that have to be claimed in your first year and cannot be changed thereafter.

With any business start up your accountant will be best placed to advise you on tax relief and/or grants.

Tax Advisor

Tax advisors can and should be used in addition to your accountant. Once your accounts have been prepared your tax advisor may be able to show you additional ways to save on your tax bill.

This in no way reflects on your accountants abilities. Your accountant prepares your annual accounts based on the information you supply. Your tax advisor will make suggestions about ways to legitimately reduce your tax liability if possible. The two can work together well to help you build the best business possible and retain as much profit as possible to go back into your business.

VPA, Fulfillment and Drop Ship Companies

I introduced you earlier in this book to the concept of working on your business not in your business. I'm sure many of you thought how the hell can I start a business and not work in it. That's where VPA, fulfillment and drop ship companies come in.

VPA (Virtual Personal Assistant)

A virtual personal assistant (VPA) is a type of call centre that takes your calls during normal office hours. They answer your calls in your business name. You spend some time training the VPA on how you would like your calls answered and how they should process each call. They act as your own personal assistant.

In my property management business the VPA answers the telephone calls, makes bookings to view properties or arranges visits to existing tenants. They chase up outstanding rents. They can deal with emergencies and ensure callouts are placed with the gas engineer or the electrician. They handle emails, snail mail and social media.

In fact, my VPA is not only my personal assistant but my receptionist and my back office support. The company provides training to three staff members to ensure I have continuous professional support for 52 weeks of the year. And all this service is provided at a fraction of the cost of an employee.

All my tenants believe there is a large professional management company looking after them and the feedback is really positive. My time spent on the telephone, writing letters and chasing up contractors has been reduced to around half an hour a day. This has freed me up to work on my business not be stuck in my business.

Fulfillment Companies

If you are setting up a business whereby the customer telephones you to place an order or places an order using the internet you can use a fulfillment company to act on your behalf to take the order, debit the customers account, send the product to the customer and send the profit to your bank account. Every step of the way they act as though they are your business. You have a unique telephone number which they answer in your business name. The invoice generated is in your name and to all intent and purposes the customer believes they are dealing direct with your business.

A fulfillment company will hold stock piles of your product and any packaging to send out to the customer once an order is placed. They will notify you when stocks are running low and you will need to replenish the stock and packaging.

The company will have a per transaction fee for answering the telephone, taking the order, sending the product to the customer, storage and paying the profit to your bank account.

It is a cost effective way of having a fully automated business without the major cost of equipment and staff.

Drop Ship Company

With a drop ship company you are selling their product. They hold the supplies and despatch them direct to the client on receiving instruction and payment from you.

Some drop ship companies will have a website link whereby they receive payment directly to the company and a commission will be paid on to you.

Other drop ship companies will expect you to deal directly with the customer. It is your job to send orders and payments to the drop ship company before they dispatch the product to the customer.

This is a very cost effective system if you do not have your own products to sell and operate through an affiliate/commission basis.

Both fulfillment companies and drop ship companies offer a great way of running a large business from home without the overheads associated with having to employ staff.

Other Options for Running Your Business

With the expansion and development of the internet and new technology it is now possible to run a business from just about anywhere in the world without the need for staff. All work can be contracted out to specialist business who operate as if they are your own business. You can have your own personal secretary – online – who will deal directly with your customers and pass the messages on to you by email so you can spend the day doing your own thing and allocate an hour a day to dealing with your emails. Once you respond the email telling the secretary what you want done or how to deal with a specific enquiry the secretary will send letters on your behalf, talk to the customer or deal with any complaint without you ever having to speak or deal directly with the customer.

You can get the accounts and book keeping records for your business completed online without ever having to visit an accountant.

You can set up a virtual office whereby all correspondence is sent and then forwarded on to you without the customer ever having to know where you live or that you are running your business from home. All telephone calls are answered by your virtual office in your name and forwarded to your mobile or specified landline. Messages can be taken and you call the customer back. This makes the company appear a larger business than it is and more professional. If you need to hold a meeting with supplies or a customer your virtual office will normally have a room you can use as required for meetings.

With the use of all these services along with fulfillment and drop ship companies your business could be dealing with millions of pounds worth of product sales a year and you never have any direct employees or stock to hold. Your business is fully automated and it is up to you how many hours you choose to work and how big or small you want your business to be.

Section 1 – Summary

When it comes to starting a business it is best to do your research thoroughly ensuring you have a plan and the right people around you.

Remember the quote – *Businesses don't plan to fail, they fail to plan.*

80% of businesses fail in the first five years of being started. Out of 100 businesses started in 2012 eighty will fail within five years. 20 businesses will continue to operate but out of those 20 another 80% will fail within the following 5 years. So in the first 10 years only four businesses will survive.

Why do only 4 businesses out of 100 make it?

There are numerous reasons. One of the main one is failing to plan. Complacency is another along with changing your business model and there are many other reasons.

I remember reading a story about a new restaurant. The owners worked hard to set up the right chef, manager; restaurant staff and create a great atmosphere. They built such a successful restaurant business with bookings having to be made months in advance. But the company became complacent. Staff changed and standards slipped. The very thing that had given them a competitive edge now let them down and the business went downhill very quickly eventually closing.

You can set up a business by subcontracting all or part of the operations to fulfilment companies, drop ship companies, virtual offices and virtual accountants, secretaries, etc. making your business seem larger than it is and more professional.

A businessman I know had a small business for cleaning yachts and boats which he ran from a bedroom in his home. To make the business appear larger than it was he obtained three 0800 numbers which were routed to the telephone in his bedroom. He placed an advertisement in a newspaper offering his services in three counties near his home. In the advert the customers from county one was told to use the first 0800 number. The customers from county two was told to use the second 0800 number and the same applied to the third county and third 0800 number. This simple action made it appear that he had offices in three counties where in fact he was still running the business from his spare bedroom at home.

The result being he picked up a massive contract for cleaning boats at shows around the country because his business appeared larger than it was.

In the next section I will take you through a step-by-step guide to building your own niche marketing business and help you avoid some of the pitfalls that other marketers, including me, have fall into.

Section 2

Step by Step Guide to Building A Niche Marketing Business

Section 2 – Introduction

When it comes to niche marketing Golf is one of my favourite subjects to explain the principal of niche marketing. So what is a niche market and why is niche marketing such a successful business model.

Definition of a Niche Market

Golf is played by millions of people all around the world. Each player has a set of golf clubs and a ball. The aim is to get around a course of 18 holes in the shortest number of strokes. Everyone has different results and different challenges. Some people are great players and some are poor players.

Remember when creating a business you are looking at problems potential customers have and the best way to solve the problem. For many golfers putting is a problem. How many golfers do you think would buy a gadget, a dvd or a book if they though it would improve their putting? The answer is a lot.

Putting is a small (niche) part of the golf game. In providing a service or information on improving your putting you are providing a service to a niche market.

Another example of niche markets is the gold rush that happened in America in the 1800's. A lot of Americans thought they could make their fortune finding gold. Most failed. The successful people during the gold rush were not those searching for gold but those businesses that supplied maps, equipment, dynamite or showed the miners where or how to mine gold.

I invest in property. To support my investment I have several businesses each of which is a niche part of the property market. I have a business for managing the properties. I have a business for providing maintenance at my properties. I have another business that provides gas, electric, phones and broadband to each property. There is yet another business that deals with eco systems and solar power. Each business is stand alone and can be sold at any time if I wanted to. Each business provides a different service and has a different function. There are still many niche businesses I can set up which are beneficial for me and other landlords within the property market the scope seems to be almost limitless. Every time I find a problem within the property market I can find a solution and another business idea.

Niche marketing is about identifying a specific problem or need your potential client has and providing a possible solution.

Think about your hobby or interest. What problems or needs can you identify and what possible solutions can you provide?

Finding Customers

If you don't have a customer you don't have a business.

In the traditional business format a business will set up it's operations, employ sales people and try to persuade the consumer to purchase the product or service. The company spends thousands or millions of pounds advertising their product and hoping they can find a customer to buy it.

In niche marketing we are first going to find the customer, find out what they need, what problems they have and then decide how we can solve those problems for them.

Have you been into a newsagent store recently? What magazines have you seen on the shelf? There a skiing, snowboarding, yachting, sewing, model engineering, racecar engineering, share market, franchising and the list goes on and on.

Each person who buys the magazine buys it for information. They may want to keep up to date with latest developments. They may want to improve their knowledge. They may have a problem and don't know how to solve it. These are ready made customers who are waiting to buy.

So how do you tap into this ready made market with harassing each customer in the shop for their information? The answer is using mailing lists.

What is a mailing list?

When ever you buy something most businesses keep a record of who you are, what you purchased and how often you purchase along with other information. From time to time you receive offers in the mail for a new product they are selling or a sale they might be running. How often do you get special offers from Sainsbury, Tesco or Asda offering you a discount if you spend x amount of pounds in their shop or online? You have become part of the mailing list of customers for that business.

My husband regularly buys products from a company called Machine Mart. We travel to their shop in Cardiff. With each purchase they ask for our address and create an invoice with our name and address. Through the purchase we have automatically been added to their mailing list.

Have you ever entered competitions? Information supplied for the competition becomes part of a mailing list.

Many businesses will use a List Broker to manage the mailing list for them.

One of the biggest companies is Hilite Direct Marketing. Check their website at www.hilitedms.co.uk it has a wealth of information. You will get an idea of the type of lists they have available.

Any list broker will have a register of the lists which they manage on behalf of companies. They will provide to you with a list of names and addresses of potential clients for a fee. The list broker will take his commission from the fee and pass the balance on to the owner of the list.

Any list purchased can only be used once. You then need to repurchase another list if you want to target the customer again. When purchasing the mailing list you will be warned that some of the names are bogus and used to ensure you are only using the customer details once. However, once a customer buys from you they become your customer and you are legally able to make them part of your own mailing list and you no longer have to pay to use the customer details again.

Once you have created you own mailing list of buying customers you can offer your list to a list broker and receive a payment if someone else wants to use your list.

Do a search on the internet and you will find numerous companies offering mailing lists for you to purchase in a wide variety of niches. You should never have a shortage of customers and customer wants. Once you have done your research and established the number of potential clients the next step is to find or create a product to sell to them.

Finding Products to Sell

Now you have a ready made customer base to try and sell your product to the next step is to find a product to sell. Here you have a choice of what type of products to sell and whether to create your own product or buy a license to sell somebody else's product.

What Type of Product to Sell?

You can sell any product you choose. Retail shops are full of businesses trying to sell one product or another. But for niche marketing the easiest and quickest products to sell is information.

Information products come in the form of books (like this one) audio such as MP3 downloads or cd's and visual such as dvd's. All of these products provide the customer with valuable information and are cheap to reproduce.

A book can be produced for a couple of pounds and sold for £47. A series of audios or visuals can be produced for around £1 per copy and sold for £997. Profits can be and usually are many more times the cost of producing the product.

If however, I had to manufacture the product – say a pair of shoes then the cost to me would be quite a lot of money. Then I would need my profit on selling the item. If the item were faulty or damaged in the post I would have to fit the bill to replace it. If the client didn't like the fit they would send the item back.

With information products they rarely get damaged, are rarely returned and offer the potential for large profits. If the quality of the product is good then the customer will keep buying from you regardless of the price charged.

Create You Own Product

It is possible to create your own products to sell. In my case I do create a lot of my own product through writing my own books and ebooks. Because I produce my own produce I also get to retain most of the profit for myself. But writing a book takes time. Producing an audio or visual product takes time. For me, I love writing and while I usually only write one book a year I still enjoy the process.

For people less inclined to create their own products there are still opportunities available to sell unique products.

Buy A Licensed Product

This is a process I use in addition to creating my own product to sell. I buy a licensed product. The type of license I am looking for allows me to rebrand a product and make it totally unique to me.

For example – I recently bought the rights to a product which included a book and 12 dvd's. Under the agreement I am able to create my own cover for the books and dvd's and give it a name totally unique to me. I can sell the product with my own brand on it making it totally unique to my business. Other people may also have a license to the product but no one can sell it using my designs. It is therefore a product totally unique to me.

I will break the product down into several parts.

- A book and 3 dvd's which I will sell for about £47.

- A series of 6 or 7 dvd's selling for about £197
- And finally the full set of dvd's along with the book for £497.

The few thousand pounds paid for the licence will generate around £20,000 income. All from a product create by someone else that I have rebranded and sold as my own.

Affiliates

The third option is to become an affiliate for a company. An example is that my books are available through Amazon books. You could open an account with Amazon to sell my books and they would pay you a commission for each book sold. This is called being an affiliate. You do your own marketing and sales online through your own websites and advertising but using a code supplied by Amazon when a customer clicks on your link to buy my books the purchases go through Amazon and you receive commission for the sale.

As an affiliate you have a ready made product with no hassles about printing, design or delivering the product. The work is all done for you. Remember in previous sections of this book I referred to drop ship companies by acting as an affiliate you are basically operating with a drop ship company.

As an affiliate you can sell any product you are not limited to just information products. For example most shops are affiliates as they sell other peoples brands. Sainsbury's sell their own brand food but they also sell many other brands. This is a form of affiliate marketing.

Rebranding

Rebranding is a simple technique that allows you to create your own unique product.

To rebrand a product you need to have a license that entitles you to do this. You can purchase numerous products such as books, dvd's, cd's etc that allow you to rename the product, put your name on the product as if you created it yourself. You design new labels for the product and then sell it as your own.

Generally, the original manufacturer has provided you the license for a one off fee and has no further interest in the product.

If you have a master resell license you can rebrand and sell the product to other niche marketers who are looking for products giving them the right to rebrand the product themselves.

Getting Started

When I first started in niche marketing I bought a product for £197.00 which allowed me to rebrand it. The product which consisted of a book and dvd. I used the website company elance to design a new front page for the book with matching dvd label. The cost was around £30. I had a digital version of the book on my computer and replaced the front page with my newly designed front page. Each time I sold the book it was produced with my unique front page and the dvd had my design on it as well.

The product was totally unique to me and I had no other competition in the market place for sales.

Equipment

It is interesting to look back at how I started this business in my spare bedroom with a computer, printer and dvd copier. When orders came in I printed the book and put it in a ring binder. Using dvd labels I printed the label and stuck it on the copied dvd which was placed inside the front cover of the folder which had a little half sleeve. The whole lot fitted into a large brown envelope and that afternoon I would go down to my local post office and send the parcels.

I then progressed to using a ring binding machine for the books which I thought looked a bit more professional. This later became a book cover binding machine which looked even more professional.

Today the fulfilment company has contractors who produce the products on demand and now they look really professional.

Basically, this story is to show you don't need much equipment to get started in a niche marketing business.

Ebooks

There are some companies who specialise in producing ebooks which you can rebrand and sell as though you have written the book yourself. All you need is to be able to design a new cover to go on the book. Then you can advertise your new ebook for sale.

A word of caution – these books are often hastily written, with poor English, bad grammar and terrible spelling. If you are going to use ebooks as one of your products it pays to edit the book and correct the mistakes.

Remember you are trying to provide a good quality product to your customer so they come back again and again to buy more products from you. Poorly produced ebooks will not only annoy your customer but will cost you future sales and credibility.

Value for Money.

The core of any business is having repeat customers. Repeat customers are those people who come back to your business and buy from you over and over again.

If you run a fish & chip shop and a customer comes in for the first time. They order cod and chips and are so pleased with the quality of the food, the amount of food and the service they received they come back a second time then a third and so on. You now have a repeat customer and as long as you continue to deliver quality food, good quantity and good service the customer will probably continue to buy from your shop. The customer has the perception of receiving value for money or more than they expected.

When you are in niche marketing you must still be able to provide the customer with perceived value for money and exceed their expectations. If the customer is delighted with what they receive they will come back again and again buying more products usually at higher prices.

If you watch an infomercial on the television they create the perception of receiving more for their money. For example on the television at the moment is an infomercial by Guthy Renker for Principal Secrets Reclaim – a skincare range of products. The infomercial claims for this type of skincare range you could easily expect to pay more than £70 in a shop but they are not going to sell it to you for that price they are going to reduce the price to just £29.99. Perception you are getting value for money. But they don't just stop their in addition they are giving you two other products free of charge just for trying the skincare range. They will enrol you free of charge into the

Principal Secret club guaranteeing you only pay £24.95 per month there after. They will automatically send you the next supply of your product every 3 months (giving them a repeat customer) and if you don't like the product they give you a full 60 day bottom of the jar, refund. So try the product for 60 days if you don't like it send it back even if the jar is empty to get a refund.

As you can see there are extras being added on to what was already deemed to be a good price for the skincare range. Will you be tempted to buy? Many are as according to their infomercial they have more than two million happy customers.

When putting your products together you need to give the customer perceived value. If the customer feels they have received good value product then they will come back and buy from you again and again.

So how do you create perceived value for your product?

Obviously, it depends on the product you are selling for example with one of my products 'How to make £30,000 a Month', I provided the customer with a book which outlined a system for making £30,000 a month. The customer also received a couple of cd's; a booklet of suggest advertisements that work (worth £9.99); free sales letters easy to amend for any product (worth £9.99); free 12 month membership to my newsletter (worth £30); a free 1 hour consultation directly with me valid for 30 days (worth £120) and a money back guarantee and all for the price of £37. Did the customer think they were getting value for money? Yes, they did and this product proved to be a good seller.

What was the cost to me?

1 x book £1.20

1 x 2 cd set 12p (6p per cd)

1 x newsletter membership – zero – the newsletter was already in production and adding extra names to the mailing list cost me nothing. At the end of the 12 months some of them started to pay the £2.50 monthly subscription.

1 x Consultation – zero – not one customer contacted me for consultation.

1 x guarantee – zero – no products were returned.

Total cost to me £1.32 plus postage and packaging (£4.95) for a product sold at £37 which the customer perceived gave them value for money.

It shouldn't cost you much to give the customer value for money. The main thing is you want the customer to be happy with what they received and you want them to come back and buy from you again. With this product around 20% of the customers signed up to my monthly newsletter. Many of the customers went on to buy more products from me. They were happy and so was I.

Understanding the Funnel Technique.

The Funnel is a sales technique used to sell more products to your customers at growing cost.

Using the chart below you can start to understand the funnel process.

Sell low priced product with 500 customers purchasing the product i.e. £37 product as show on previous pages

Offer higher value product to the 500 customers at the cost of £147. Number of customers responding 200

Offer another higher value product at say £697 to the remain 200 customer uptake of customers buying 75

Offer another higher value product at £1997 to remain 75 customers of which 30 take up the offer.

Using 'How to Make £30,000 in A Month' let's study how the funnel system works and how you profit from it.

In the chart the first sales were for £37 (a book and two cd's plus added bonuses) with 500 customers responding. Your sales = £18,500. Cost to you £1.32 x 500 = £660. Your profit is £17840.

You now have on your mailing list 500 customers who want to make £30,000 a month. They are customers who have liked your product and are starting to trust you. You now have a set of 6 dvd's that you are going to offer to them for £147. You send the offer out a few weeks after the first purchase. The number of customers responding to is 200. Your sales are £29,400 the cost to you is still 6p per dvd so a set of 6 dvd's will cost you 36 pence and times that by 200 customers total cost £72. Your total profit is £29,328.

As the product got higher the number of customers responding to the higher price gets lower but you still have 200 customers. So you now offer them another higher cost product.

This time you have a set of 6 cd's, 15 dvd's and a manuscript of all the cd's. You are also going to include a book by 4 well known niche marketing gurus showing them the systems they can use to make money. There will be a selection of sales letters used by the gurus and a licence to a product the customer can brand themselves giving them a unique product they can sell. The total cost this time is £697. This time only 75 customers will buy the product. Total sales £52,275. The total cost to you is 75 books at £1.20 = £90. Cost of 6 cd's at 6p each or 36p a set is £27 and the dvd set is £67.50 total cost £184.50. Your total profit is £52090.50

The last step is to offer a seminar where you personally take the customer through the steps outlined in the products to which 30 customers take up the offer. Total sales are £59910. Your cost is hiring the hall at £100 for the day. Customers bring their own refreshments and your profits are £59810.

So you have paid £1000 for a licence and then breaking the product up into different size parcels to sell your customer through the funnel technique you have made a total profit of £159,068.

You have a cash rich business with happy customers willing to spend money time and again with you.

Added Bonuses

A lot of people panic about added bonuses. I regularly get asked at seminars what are added bonuses?

What are added bonuses? – they are simply something you give the customer in addition to your normal product that gives benefit to the customer and confidence that they can trust you. Remember, this may be the first time the customer has dealt with you. How do they know they can trust you?

Your first bonus is to give a 30 day no questions asked money back guarantee. To date, I have not had one product returned. But if I did get a product returned I would willingly give the customer their money back less the postage costs.

The second bonus I give to customers is a free personal consultation with me. The consultation is via email and I will answer any questions the customer wants up to the value of one hour of my time. The consultation is valid for 15 days from the date of purchase of the product. So far, not one person has sent me an email but from the customer perspective this is value for money as they get the opportunity to discuss the contents directly with me if needed.

The third bonus I give customers is a free subscription for a period of time to a newsletter based on the subject of the product I am selling after which time they are automatically subscribed to my newsletter. Auto responders are good for this as you can preset the newsletters to go to the customer. To set this up I include a registration form or a link to a website and ask for standing order details advising the customer their standing order will commence on a specific date unless they give notice they wish to cancel the subscription. A free newsletter is included with the product so the customer is aware of the information contained in the newsletter. The newsletter then becomes an ongoing product sold every month. I have several newsletters for several niches each producing a nice monthly income.

Other bonuses – a transcript of a cd or dvd. If you listen to the cd or watch the dvd you can write a transcript. If you don't want to do it yourself you can outsource the task through companies online such as elance.

A booklet with a summary of the key points on the dvd is also a helpful bonus. They are easy to put together. While you watch a dvd take a few notes and put this in a little booklet. It doesn't need to be detailed. You are just providing a few key points from the dvd.

For some of my products I supply a few sales letters. Writing a sales letter is one of the most difficult things someone new in the business will struggle with. Giving them some ready made sales letters takes the strain off the customer. If you aren't confident in writing sales letters there are some readily available on the internet as free downloads which you can easily print or copy to a dvd.

For several years I have written 'how to' books covering a range of topics. They are available at various low cost prices and can easily be included as a bonus item or as part of a product you are putting together.

Hopefully by now you are getting the idea. Simple things, easily sourced add up to valuable bonuses when putting your sales pitch together.

More Information on Finding A Product to Sell

If you've managed to get this far in the book you are probably getting really worried about finding a product. So let's put your mind at rest and show you how easy it is to discover what are the best topics to cover and what products you should be selling.

We've already covered that the best products to sell are information products. These are products in digital format i.e. books; ebooks; videos; dvd; mp3 etc. They cost very little to reproduce and sell at a handsome profit. But you are probably more concerned about the topic offering the best chances of success. To discover the best products you need access to an internet and do some research.

Option 1 – Affiliate Products

One of the best sites to find affiliate products is Clickbank – www.clickbank.com they have literally thousands of products you can sign up to sell. They offer help centres to get you started. This really is a quick and easy way to get started for little or no cost.

Associate Programs is another good website with lots of products and information for the beginner. Their website is www.associateprograms.com

Other websites to look at

www.affiliatedatabase.com

www.associateprograms.com/directory/

www.associatesearch.com/

www.freeassociateprograms.com/

This is just a sample of some of the affiliate programme websites available. Do your own search on the internet and find out how many sites and directories there are.

Remember with affiliate programs all you are doing is redirecting customers to an existing website. The sales pitch is all done the site is 100% up and running. Your job is to redirect as many potential customers to the site using your unique code. If the customer buys you get paid a commission.

Option 2 – Resell, Reprint or Master Resell Licenses

Again you need access to the internet and put resell, reprint or master resell licenses in the search. You will find a list of products available. Do your research carefully. If you see the words 'get-rich quick' avoid it. You are looking for products you can sell a customer not get rich quick scams.

You want a professional looking product not shoddy quick type products or dvds. The poorer the quality the less you will be able to ask for the product and the more time you waste getting no-where. With quality products you can ask quality prices.

Option 3 – Finding Product Developers

This is often easier than it sounds. There are people who enjoy producing products such as books, dvds etc. but have absolutely no idea how to go about marketing a product.

One of the easiest ways is to collect junk mail. After a few months contact the seller and offer to market their product to your customers. You can offer to pay a licensing fee. You can offer a Joint Venture (more about this later in the book) or you can simply offer to sell on a commission basis.

Another way is to advertise for products. Place an advertisement online line and/or in newspapers and see what response you can get.

Option 4 – Product Finders

Product Finders are people who already own the rights to products but have so many there is no possible way they can market everything they own. Product Finders are usually more than happy to sell a license to you. They may offer you a joint venture or they may allow you to sell the product on a commission basis. When using a product finder ask how much marketing they have done on this product. You may find you have a brand new unique product to start selling or a product they haven't marketed for several years which can be revamped and made into a new unique product.

Option 5 – Me

Put me down as your fifth option to finding products to sell. I have books, ebooks and mp3 products for which the licenses can be bought.

In addition I have access to product finders – just let me know how much you are willing to pay for a license and I can find out what is available within your price range. Bear in mind that licenses start around £200 and will go anything up to £100,000+. You will need to be very specific with what you can afford when setting up your niche marketing business and realistic on what you expect to receive for the money being spent.

Email: info@karennewton.co.uk

Advertising

There are many books written about advertising by people more expert in the field than I am so I am just going to cover the techniques I have used that have been successful for me. I leave it up to you to decide if you want to learn more about this field and/or start with some simple cost effective ideas that I use.

Mailing list – this is your most effective way of advertising your product. Earlier in the book we discussed how you can start you business buying a mailing list. Once the customer has bought your product they become part of your own mailing list. Don't underestimate the value of your mailing list. These are proven customers willing to spend money with you.

Website – set your product up so it can be ordered directly from a website. It is amazing the number of sales that are made during the night hence we hear the expression frequently about making money while you sleep. Websites are not expensive to set up. I buy .co.uk domain names for around £3.50 or £10 for a .com domain name. The domain names are renewed annually or two yearly. The company provides free websites with each domain purchased.

Capture or Squeeze Pages – is a box that opens when someone clicks on your website requesting they supply you with their name, email address and/or phone number. Many people are reluctant to provide phone numbers so don't make it compulsory as you could loose a potential customer. Capturing names and email addresses gives you another way of building your mailing list.

Newspaper Advertising – placing an ad in a local newspaper is relatively cheap and a way of directing people to your website. If you try advertising in magazines or national newspapers the costs can be fairly high for little or no replies.

Google Ads – can give your website more prominence but be careful about the cost per ad. It is easy to run up high advertising costs which are outside your control. Put a limit on how much you are willing to spend.

Facebook – a fan page for your product is a must these days. Get friends and family to like your page. Advertising is quite effective but again like google ads it is too easy to run up expensive advertising costs so ensure you place a limit on how much you are willing to spend.

Twitter – its amazing how effective twitter is for building a product or business brand. It's free and a tweet or two a day will soon have loads of followers and potential customers.

Blogs – fantastic way of promoting your product and referring customers to your website. Link them in automatic update on to social media sites such as facebook, twitter, linkedin, google+ etc.

Ezine Articles – become an expert writer about your niche. If your articles are good enough they can be picked up by newspapers and magazines looking to fill editorial space in their publication. Each article published on ezine has a resource box where you write a little about yourself, your product and your website. Ezines are good for building credibility.

Sales Pitch

Writing a sales letter is not as difficult as you think. If you can write a letter in a style similar to that of writing to a best friend then you can easily write a sales letter that will generate good sales.

The sales letter you send to your potential customer or the sales pitch on your website is the make or break of the sale. There are some tricks of the trade that increase your sales responses 30 – 50%. If you have a turnover of £10,000 it would increase your total sales by £3000 - £5000 per product.

One gentleman that I consider to be one of the great sales copy writing is Ted Nicholas. He once told me that great sales copy took 16 – 20 pages. Ted is known as the million pound copywriter so I'm not about to argue with his concepts.

I once did a training course with him which covered the best words to use in your sales copy. Afterwards the structure of my sales copy changed and the results I got improved incredibly. So investing a little time and money into improving your skills in copy writing will pay you back over and over again with increase sales and profit.

One of the products I used to sell was how to write sales letters. I still have a few copies available. You can purchase a copy direct from me on info@karennewton.co.uk The price is £17.00 for digital copy and £27.00 plus postage and packaging of £4.95 for a hard copy.

If you don't want to write your own sales copy then elance will have people willing to do this for you at a reasonable price.

Once you have the sales letter you can reproduce this onto your website. Don't forget to put links on your website for payment and for capturing names and emails addresses.

Accepting Payments

There are many ways of accepting payments depending on how your business is set up. Below are a few scenarios to help you along the way.

Affiliates – as an affiliate you are directing customers to an existing website set up by the supplier of the product. You have a code embedded in your website or advert and this lets the supplier know it was you who redirected the customer to them. As an affiliate you do not need to be able accept payments. You are paid commission by the supplier of the product.

Drop Ship Companies – when using drop ship companies the same applies as if you were an affiliate. Normally, you are redirecting a customer to a specific website to purchase the product. Or, you may have your own look alike website which is already set up to accept payments without you needing to do anything. With drop ship companies you receive commission on your sales.

Fulfilment Companies – they handle everything for you and will set up everything you need to accept payments from the customer. They will debit their fees and then pay the remaining balance to your bank account.

Paypal – one of the largest companies who will allow you to accept payment through a website. Normally there is no fee for setting the system up. There are fees payable on a percentage basis of payments made. This is debited directly from the payment before it is credited to your account.

Another benefit of paypal is if you are taking orders over the telephone you can accept payments and process them through your computer instantly while the customer is on the telephone. You know instantly if the payment is accepted or declined. – Ideal if you want to reduce costs and run your business from home until it has grown to a level whereby you would be better served using a fulfilment company.

Clickbank – if you set up a clickbank account, clickbank will process transactions for you through your website and pay you either by direct credit to your bank account or by cheque.

World Pay and 1st Shopping Cart are other companies that offer payment processing for your website. I have no experience with either of these companies so cannot comment on there services or fees. I recommend doing your own research.

Mobile Phones – with the development of smartphones it is now possible to accept credit card payments via your mobile phone. Apple, Blackberry and Android phones each have their own systems. I recommend checking with your mobile phone supplier for which system works best with your mobile phone.

Intuit GoPayment is available on most phones. It is an app that allows the customer to enter card details via your phone.

InnerFence is a card terminal that plugs into your iphone and along with an app allows you to process card transactions.

Barclays – have pingit which once the customer is registered with them they can send to any other mobile phone number also registered with them. The customer doesn't need to be a Barclays customer.

There are literally numerous ways to accept payments to your business without the cost of using a bank merchant. Banks will supply you with the facilities to accept credit/debit card payments via a terminal. You will have seen them in most shops. The bank usually charges fees on a monthly basis whether or not you make any sales.

The best advice is to shop around and find the cheapest ways of accepting payment at the start of building your business. You don't want to waste your profit on charges for payment services that many people don't or won't use.

Joint Ventures

We've touched on the subject of joint ventures earlier in the book so let's go into a bit more detail about them now.

A Joint Venture (JV) is simply partnering with someone else who can compliment your business and help you move it forwarded. It is a win/win situation for both parties. For example you have built you customer base in a golfing niche. You find a product to sell that you think is so great you can't pass the opportunity up but it is not suitable to your golfing niche customers. You now need a new customer base suitable for this product. You know someone who has the perfect customer base for your to good to pass up product.

You contact the owner of the customer base and ask if you can sell your product to his customers in exchange you offer the owner a share of the profits. The split depends on what both of you agree is a fair split.

This works the other way as well, you have a customer base but no product to sell. Find someone who has a product that suits your customer base and offer them a joint venture.

There are some people who may have developed a fantastic product but are absolutely useless at marketing. Offer a joint venture on the product or offer to buy a master license for product. They received a fee for the license and you are then free to market it to your customers.

Seminars

Your customer now trusts you and the products that you are selling so the next step is offer them a seminar. While this may sound scary it is actually quite simple and very lucrative.

For an example let's use the subject of this book that of niche marketing. We already have an established customer base of people who are buying our products on niche marketing. So we send them an invite to a seminar.

We book a room and invite a few other people who sell niche marketing products to be guest speakers at the event. The customer pays to attend the seminar and once your costs are deducted the remaining balance is your profit.

Example: My local hotel provides conference rooms for up to 500 customers and charges £27.00 per person which includes morning tea, lunch, afternoon tea, water and mints. The price includes all the facilities you need to run the seminar such as the room hire, projectors, overheads, wi-fi and pens and paper for the attendees. The hotel will also set all this up for you so all you have to do is get people to the venue.

Depending on the number of guest speakers you have how much do you think you're customers would pay to attend this prestigious event £50, £100, £500?

Here are some projected profits based on what you would charge for a customer to attend a seminar.

Customer pays £50 - your net profit per customer is £23 x 500 customers = £11,500.00

Customer pays £100 – your net profit per customer is £73 x 500 customers = £36,500.00

Customer pays £500 – your net profit per customer is £473 x 500 customers = £236,500.00

Now you see these figures think about the last seminar you attended and what price you paid for tickets to attend it. Here are some seminar invites I've received recently and the price for tickets to attend:-

- A Share market trading seminar £595 per person for one day
- A Buy-to-Let property seminar, £325 per person for one day
- A Spreadbetting seminar £2995 per person for one day (based on our hotels figures of £27 per person, this seminar may have netted the host of the seminar £1.4 million for a one day seminar)

Now you should be starting to see how lucrative seminars can be. But you have to build trust and credibility with your customers before you can run a seminar. If your customers don't know you, your guest speakers or your products then why should they attend the seminar.

Seminar Product Sales

By organising a seminar we are providing our guest speakers with a ready made audience of customers who have a track record of buying niche marketing products. Our guest speakers are free to sell their products at the seminar. Usually the guest speaker will talk about their experiences with their business. They then talk about the product they are trying to sell and offer seminar only special deals. There is usually a break between speakers so customers can go and purchase the product if they want to.

Some guest speakers are happy with the profits they make on their product sales and will not ask a fee for speaking at the event. Some speakers will want a fee and also to be able to sell their products. In some circumstances you can organise a Joint Venture where you pay a fee for the speaker in return they give you a percentage of the product sales.

Recording A Seminar

As the organiser of the seminar you can take the opportunity to record the event. The video recording becomes a product your can sell. For instance, you can sell an edited highlights dvd of the event. Every attendee at the event has the opportunity to purchase a copy at a special seminar only price. The dvd is sent out to the customer a few days later and you have a ready made customer base for further marketing.

If half your customers bought a highlights package at a show special of £19.99 plus £4.95 postage and packaging and it costs you 6p to produce the dvd and say £1.25 to post how much would your profit be?

If you can't find a calculator to work it out yourself here's the answer. Net profit per dvd £23.63 x 250 orders = £5907.50

A few weeks later you produce a series of dvd's of all the speakers at the event and offer that to your ready made customer base using your funnel marketing techniques.

Section 2 Summary

Now you have an outline of a simple money making business known as niche marketing. It is easy to set up with very little cost. You can contract out most of the work relating to the business through Virtual Personal Assistants, Fulfillment Centres or Drop Shipping.

You can sell products which are unique by creating your own product or obtaining licenses that allow you to rebrand the product. Or you can become an affiliate for someone elses product.

As you build your reputation and trust with your customer you can add lucrative seminars.

Once your systems are in place the time involved in running this business is only a couple of hours a week or month depending on how much money you want to make.

Section 3

Other Niche Business

Section 3 Introduction

In Section 1 of this book we looked at business in general. We covered how to work on the business not in the business. By working on the business you are able to look from the outside at the best way to grow your business.

Instead of working in the business we talked about using contractors to fill certain roles within the company such as virtual personal assistants, call centres, fulfilment centres and drop ship companies.

All these services allow you to grow your business without having to employ staff or have the hassles associated with employing staff. In addition it allows you to grow your business without being restricted by the costs as services are supplied on a pay as you go basis.

In Section 2 we looked specifically at information products for niche marketing and the potential to create a high cash producing business.

In Section 3 we'll look at some of the different types of niche business that I operate. Each one will be covered in some detail. Each will hopefully, provide you with some idea for your own niche business.

Richard Branson is one of the more famous entrepreneurs in Britain. The last I read he had over 300 companies. He found a problem and he set about trying to provide a solution to those problems and in doing so created over 300 companies. He is a perfect example of someone who works on his business not in his business. It would be physically impossible for him to work in all his businesses. He has set his businesses up so they run without him. He created the Virgin brand using his flamboyant nature as a marketing tool to draw attention to his business. He has become the public figurehead but he still has over 300 companies that operate with little input from him.

Using Richard Branson and the Virgin model you can also create many businesses bringing in many avenues of income providing you with great wealth.

So think about the problems you can see and how you can go about solving those problems.

Now let's look at the problems I've identified so far and how I've built businesses to solve those problems.

Rental Property

The Problem

Councils have traditionally provided housing in their local area. With the introduction of new regulations on housing standards and more maintenance needed at each property many councils could not afford to look after their existing properties. In addition, because their funds were being drained by the maintenance costs they could not afford to purchase new properties.

The councils were in a no win situation because 'right to buy' was seeing their property stock going down while demand for properties was going up. The cost of maintenance forced on them through new regulations meant they had no money to buy new houses. Governments were reducing the amount of funding available to councils as they tried to bring their budgets under control.

Housing Associations found themselves in a similar situation. They had relied on government funding to purchase new properties but this was also reduced due to budget controls forced on governments. Housing Associations were looking for alternative ways to increase the housing they had available and to earn additional income to cover the loss of government funding.

The Solution

Private landlords have become very important source of housing in the UK. In come regions there are more privately owned rental properties than council and housing association properties. Private Landords are buying and supplying housing which the councils and housing associations can't provide and don't have the funding to provide.

While there has been much negative publicity around buy-to-let landlords the reality is if they did not step in and provide additional housing to the market then many more people would be homeless as governments, councils and housing associations just don't have the funding to buy or maintain these properties.

The Business Opportunity

I saw houses that had been sat empty for many years. One house I bought had been empty for 45 years, another for 5 years. I built a niche business buying run down properties. I renovate them and turn them back into habitable houses which can be rented.

Property Management

The problem

I had a business buying and renovating run down properties. I did not particularly want to get into the lettings side of the business so I used several different lettings agencies. I was very disappointed with the services provided and the costs charged and the quality of tenants provided. When there was a problem with rent arrears or damage the problem was handed back to me to sort out.

I decided to manage my own properties. This was fine when I had a few properties but as the portfolio grew so did the amount of hours needed to manage the properties to the extent that I was no longer able to buy and renovate any other properties.

Another problem I noticed was the increasing number of 'accidental landlords' people who have become landlords because they were unable to sell the property they owned and for one reason or another were left with no alternative but to rent their property. They have no knowledge of the regulations concerning rental properties

The Solution

The solution was pretty obvious I needed to find someone I could trust who would run the properties to the standard and service level I required for my properties. They would also provide cost effective management and administration of the properties.

The Business Opportunity

If I had my own property management company I could control the way the business operated and the quality of service provided. I could market the services to other landlords. I built a niche property management company that along with managing properties also provides admin, accountancy and legal services to landlords.

The business has been set up as a franchise with each franchisee having a geographical area to run their business. The business systems operate within my specification. The costs have been reduced to a minimum for both the landlord and tenant being more cost effective than traditional agencies. Support services are provided to each franchisee so they are free to concentrate on the management of each property.

Franchises are available in various towns and cities throughout England and Wales visit www.tirokapms.co.uk for further information.

Property Maintenance

The problem

Legislation requires regular gas safety checks and electrical inspections. Specialised qualified tradesmen are required to carry out this work. They are in high demand and getting a tradesman within a reasonable time often proves difficult.

Other maintenance is required at properties and issues can range from a leaky roof to a leaky pipe. Inventories at properties identify areas where some tenants fail to maintain a lawn or garden, clean windows, clean ovens etc. Companies are required to fill these roles and again it is difficult to find a company who can provide the service within a reasonable time.

The Solution

Have a team of qualified tradesmen to cover the specialist work and a handyman who can cover other non-specialised services

The Business Opportunity

If I had my own staff dedicated to serving my properties then the downtime associated with waiting for tradesmen would no longer exist. It would also be more cost effective to run my own team of tradesmen.

I built a niche maintenance business, which I have franchised and modelled on the successful system for the property management company. This provides ready access to tradesmen when needed to work on the properties for myself and the other landlords.

The business can also provide its services to general customers.

New franchises will be available for this business from 2014 throughout England and Wales please visit our website www.tirokamaintenance.co.uk for further information and details of when the new regions will be available.

Utilities

The problem

We all need utilities in the form of gas, electric, water etc. Gas and Electric are dominated by the six major companies who provide lousy service at exorbitant prices. No matter how hard you try to save money the costs just seem to go up every year.

The Solution

The only solution was to become a hermit living in a cave or find a cheaper supplier for utilities.

The Business Opportunity

I found a network marketing business that guarantees to supply gas and electric cheaper than the big six companies. I built a niche business supplying gas and electric to my rental properties. Other services provided include phones and broadband. Most of my tenants are happier because their gas and electric is cheaper. I'm happy because I earn residual commission on the utilities used at each of my properties guaranteed for as long as I own the properties.

Network marketing is a bit like franchising in that each distributor builds there own business as big or small as they choose and I earn money for helping them to build it.

If you would like more information about network marketing then visit the link below

http://www.telecomplus.co.uk/biz/videodir/home.taf?exref=J1 9811

Property Niche Business

As you can see from the examples on the previous pages, I have built several niche businesses all of which are based in the housing market. I've identified problems and come up with possible solutions to those problems. I have found a group of people who have liked the solutions and decided to join with me and become business owners in my ventures. In other words they are doing joint ventures with me. We are all in a win/win situation. I've found a way of solving my problems. They have found a way of having access to proven business models. We are all able to serve an increasing number of customers that we could not have managed had we been on our own.

The thing I like about these joint ventures are the people I work with, who are from different walks of life. Some were on benefits and looking for a way to move forward. Some are business owners who found a way to increase their income working part time around their existing commitments and others are in jobs they want to get away from and are building businesses that will eventually allow them to leave their jobs. However, they all have one thing in common they own a niche business. They all see the opportunities available to them.

What can you see?

Other Types of Niche Business

Not all my niche businesses are based on property, below are some of the other businesses I run which are aimed at specific niches.

Publishing

I have three niche publishing businesses.

Business 1 – publishes my books such as this one. The books are published in digital or paperback and sold through different outlets such as Amazon, Smashwords, Google and Kobo.

Business 2 – works with new previously unpublished authors. It provides the opportunity to have books reviewed, recommendations made with a view to getting the work published through our business.

Business 3 – this one is the traditional information product niche marketing which I have covered in Section 2 of this book. I have books, dvds and cds which are marketed online and processed through a fulfilment centre.

Finance

I have a few niche businesses that operate in the financial markets. Two of the businesses are:

Business 1 – is a lending business which provides loans to individuals and small businesses who can't obtain money through banks. No, these are not payday loans. They are FSA approved loans for terms up to 5 years and known in the industry as P2P lending.

Business 2 – Angel Investing is where capital is provided to new start up businesses or existing businesses who want to expand and in exchange for the investment I receive shares in the company. I have the opportunity to keep my shares in the business and receive an income from them once the company becomes profitable or I can sell the shares and hopefully make a profit.

Section 3 Summary

There are many niche business opportunities. Just look around and you will find successful business working in a niche market.

Most niche businesses can be started from home and expanded to other premises as or when the business grows. Some businesses can be run from the spare bedroom indefinitely regardless of how much profit they make.

I mentioned earlier Deirdre Bounds who started a gap year travel business which she sold for an eight figure sum. The niche business was started in her spare bedroom.

In Section 2 of this book we covered information products – I know a couple of people in this industry who have made £20 million + from this niche business which they run from a spare bedroom.

In the Utilities network marketing business a friend of mine makes £30,000+ per month from a business he runs from his spare bedroom.

Hopefully you get the picture almost any business can be started from the spare bedroom of your home so you don't need to fork out a lot of money for premises to get started. All you need is the drive and persistence to run a successful business.

There is definitely a business out there for everyone. Identify problems, come up with ways to solve them then decided which will make a good business opportunity for you.

I hope this book has given you some ideas and you have discovered a niche business opportunity that suits you. I hope it's a business that can be started for little cash and operated from your spare bedroom; a business that can be built around the demands of your existing job; a business that will eventually provide an income so you can leave your job; a business that can provide you with the opportunity to create wealth and a new lifestyle.

I wish you good luck with your new venture

About The Author

Born in London, raised in South Wales, part educated in France and having lived in New Zealand and Australia, Karen has developed a unique understanding of world economies.

Karen's employment background started in the UK with Inland Revenue where she worked as a clerical assistant on PAYE before moving to Schedule D to specialise in taxes for self-employed and corporations.

Moving to New Zealand Karen went into banking. She worked in various positions within the bank moving to new positions through promotion. Areas covered included Accounting; Teller; International; Training; Visa and Corporate Lending. Karen was an Assistant Manager when she left the bank to move into her own business.

During her time in New Zealand she was joint owner of several businesses with her husband as well as individual owner of her own businesses. The businesses included Fire Protection; Security; Electrical Contracting; Air Conditioning. She created history by becoming the first female member of the Fire Protection Contractors Association and went on to become its chairperson, which at the time had a constitutional maximum term of two years. This was amended to allow her to continue in the role for a further five years. In her own right she had a Cosmetic Company and Writing Business

Attending night classes at University in New Zealand Karen studied, Commercial Law; Accounting; Business Management and Quality Management.

Karen developed her interest in writing and wrote advertorials for the local daily newspaper, Hawkes Bay Today; Karting articles for Motorsport NZ and Karting NZ; and numerous articles sold to various magazines.

Returning to the UK in 2000, Karen worked for a recycling consortium as Administrator; Retail Manager and Quality Manager while continuing to build her investment portfolio. Being made redundant twice she eventually retired to concentrate on managing and building her investments.

Today Karen is the owner of several businesses including Property Rentals; Lending; Publishing; Niche Marketing; Mentoring and Network Marketing. She has investments in Property, Shares, Bonds and Commodities.

To find out more about Karen visit her website www.karennewton.co.uk

Or you can follow Karen on twitter @newydd105

Bonus Chapters

In the following pages you will find some bonus chapters from a selection of books by Karen all of which are available in paperback or digital format from Amazon books.

We hope you have enjoyed this book and enjoy the following books.

Surviving 2013 – A Financial Guide (Bonus Chapter)

Financial Pyramid

I use a Financial Pyramid as a way of ensuring a balanced array of investments. In the first section of this book I spoke about investment cycles. Cycles cover every type of investment and indicate when an investment product is in a growth or decline period.

The interesting thing about cycles is that investments don't all go up together or down together. They move at different times and for different lengths of time. For example in the UK, property had a boom from 2000 up to 2007 and has been in decline since. For the Gold Cycle, Gold has been steadily going up for over a decade.

The benefit of understanding cycles is to buy when the investment is at its lowest. This is when the investment is usually at its cheapest point. It's like going shopping during the sales. You are looking for the best deal at the cheapest price. The investments I look at are usually out of favour with journalist and financial advisors as my feeling is once you start reading about the investment in the newspaper then the best money has already been made in the investment. On the other hand I try to get out of a market when it is at its peak. I'm not always as successful as I could be. In 2001 I started buying shares as the share market was low at around 3200 for the FTSE100. In 2005, I thought the market had reached the top of the cycle and I sold all my shares for a healthy profit. I was wrong in my judgement and the share market continued to climb for a long time. There was a lot more money that could have been made. The thing is not to get too greedy. I had made a healthy profit so there was really nothing to complain about.

When I start reading things like property is going up and now is the time to buy, I know that now is the time for me to stop buying property and start looking at a different investment in a different cycle period. Once the masses start getting into an investment the opportunity to make large gains has gone. I also know it won't be too long before the bubble bursts. When I hear comments like the housing market is about to collapse I take it with a pinch of salt. Do my own research and buy when the figures make the most sense for my investment.

During the time I was buying property I frequently heard comments such as get out now the housing market is about to collapse. 'It is a sellers market rather than a buyers market. You are best to wait until the market changes.' If I had listened to every bit of advice offered during this time I would never have bought any property. In the song 'The Gambler' by Kenny Rogers the words are 'You gotta to know when to hold them, know when to fold them. Know when to walk away and know when to run.' The point there is YOU have to know not you have to listen to someone else telling you when to walk away or run. So don't listen to TV channels or newspapers when they advise the next best investment is xyz or your investment is about to collapse. Do your own research and have confidence in your decisions.

I like to vary my investments so when one is down in value another is up in value. This means I don't have exposure to just one area. For this reason I collect data on the investments I hold. I create my own cycle information from the data I collect. I have a very simple spread sheet in Microsoft Excel and create graphs from the data.

I keep a gold cycle spread sheet and earlier this year gold reached around $1800 then moved back. I heard stories from everywhere saying gold had peaked and was on the way back done. My cycle charts told me differently and I continued to buy gold. My profits increased over the new couple of months.

Different financial institutions keep their own records and I have found that keeping my own gives me more confidence in my decisions based on my information. It is the same with the Financial Pyramid. Other financial institutions have their own version of a financial pyramid and I have my own. The one below is my version. You may like to look at other financial pyramids and as you build your knowledge try putting together your own version of the pyramid. But for the rest of this section we are going to work on my financial pyramid.

Building Your Pyramid

With the exception of the top of the pyramid – the section called Speculation – I try to add to each of the other four sections every month. This way I haven't concentrated on building just one part of the pyramid. I have used a balanced approach and spread my investments over various sections.

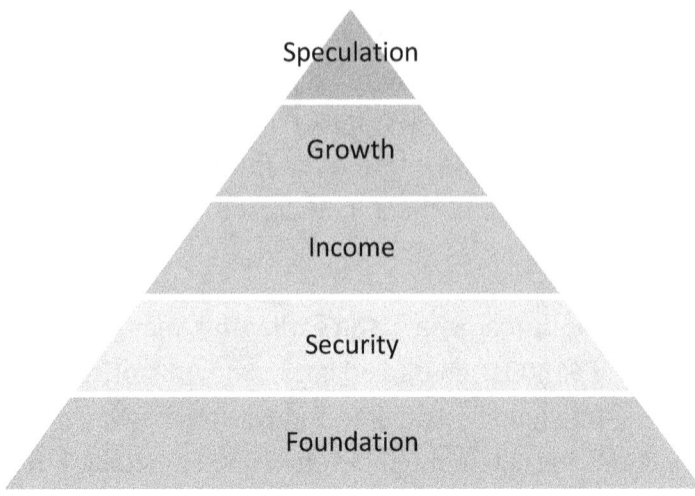

What Makes Up My Financial Pyramid

Please don't confuse the word pyramid with a multitude of fraudulent schemes that are out there in the world of money. I have used a pyramid or triangle shape as being the norm in financial sector and because it is a very solid shape and our aim is to build a solid financial structure for our futures.

Foundation

In the foundation of my pyramid I have commodities. The commodities I currently hold are Gold, Silver and Copper. You can add other commodities (such as platinum, palladium, nickel, oil, gas etc.) or reduce them depending on their position in their investment cycle. For me I try to hold in the region of 5% - 10% of my wealth in commodities. As a commodity goes up in price I use the strategy of doubling my money whereby once a commodity has doubled in value I sell off half to recoup the investment I made. Holding onto the other half if I think it will still go up in value and buy another commodity currently out of favour and at the lower end of its investment cycle. I am still trying to keep the balance of 5%-10% of my wealth in commodities.

Security

The security section is as it says my security. In this section I hold cash deposits this is money in the bank. Money invested in ISA and SIPP and government bonds. These are all fairly stable types of investments that have government guarantee if anything goes wrong with the organisation my money is held with. Banks now have £85,000 government guarantee per banking institution. You can hold up to one million in government bonds and are guaranteed the return of your money should there be any problems.

Income

This is the section that creates my income for the year. In this section I have businesses that I own outright and provide me with an income through wages or dividends. I have business in which I am a silent partner and receive a dividend from the investment. I have residual income which is generated through my network marketing business. I have royalties which are paid from my books. I receive rental income from the properties that I own. I have what is known as Blue Chip shares that pay a regular dividend and I run a lending portfolio and receive monthly interest from this.

Growth

In the growth section my investments are aimed at producing capital growth in the future rather than a regular income. So in this section I have investments in companies that qualify through the governments Enterprise Investment Scheme (EIS). I invest in small companies listed on the stock exchange that are reinvesting all their money back into the business for future growth. I invest in exploration companies for gas, oil, gold etc.

Angel Investing is another growth potential where I supply money and/or expertise to a business in exchange for a negotiated return sometime in the future.

Property forms part of the growth section as I hope property will over a long period of time rise in value. When buying property my intention is not to sell. I am investing in property for the long term. The property that the Duke of Westminster holds has been in his family for generations. He may have sold some property and bought others but the Duke of Westminster holds an awful lot of property in the Westminster borough. It is my plan to be able to pass my properties on to my daughter and while I never say never, my intention is to hold the property indefinitely and be able to pass it on to future generations.

Speculation

This section is dedicated mainly to Spreadbetting. This is something I use very rarely. Because I trade very rarely I have yet to find a system producing a winning streak. Although I don't trade them I would include Forex, futures and options in this section.

So now you have my interpretation of a Financial Pyramid and I hope this gives you an overview of how I build up my overall portfolio of investments. Now let's look at some of these investments in more detail.

Paperback Version

http://www.amazon.co.uk/Surviving-Financial-Guide-Karen-Newton/dp/1480117161

Digital Version

http://www.amazon.co.uk/Surviving-2013-Financial-Guide-ebook/dp/B009R3T66K

Make A Living From Property (Bonus Chapter)

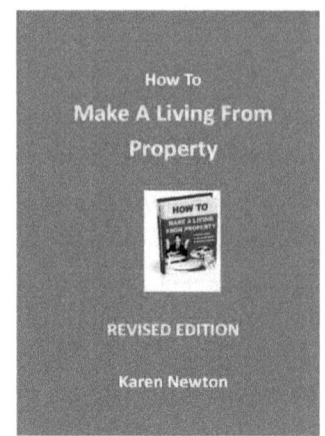

Finding A Suitable Property

There are many different types of properties to invest in. Some people choose commercial, some people like apartments while others like new build houses. There are overseas investment properties. As for me, I like existing structurally sound properties needing interior renovation.

My criteria is:

- Existing 2, 3, 4 or 5 bedroom houses
- Structurally sound
- The worst house in the street
- Good opportunity for capital growth
- Good rental opportunities
- Financials Stack Up

Let's look at each item of my criteria in more detail.

1. Existing 2, 3, 4 or 5 bedroom houses

I like existing houses of any size. Two bedroom houses suit either single or married couples. Larger houses cater for couples with children. In most cases I am looking for a tenant that is likely to be more stable. Generally, the more children the more likely the tenant will stay for some time. When apartments are involved frequently the tenant will move around and I like to keep things simple. I don't want to be dealing with new tenants and tenancies every six months.

I like existing properties because they are already built and I know what I am getting. With a 'new build' you are buying off plan. You have to imagine what the property will look like when it is finished. You have to make a down payment which ties up your money until the property is built. This could be months or even years before the property is ready. This is too slow for me. I like to see my return on investment quickly.

Existing houses allows me to assess the neighbourhood to see if it is likely the property will rent quickly. Is it a good neighbourhood, close to schools and shops? Is it a deprived area with unruly behaviour, break in etc. where tenants would prefer not to live.

2. Structurally Sound

When looking at a house I don't care what condition the interior is in. It is quite easy and fairly cheap to put in new kitchens, new bathrooms and repair and decorate the interior. This type of property can be made ready for a tenant to move into within a reasonable time. Reducing the time my property is vacant. On the other hand, if there is damage to a roof or the exterior walls then I don't know how much other damage is involved and this could become quite costly. I would need specialist tradesmen and I would have little or no control on how quickly the work will be done. My aim is to turn a property around very quickly, get it tenanted with the least amount of downtime possible, after all, every day a property is empty it is costing me money instead of making me money.

3. The worst house in the street

One of my first questions is how much are other houses selling for in the street. The property I am looking at normally needs a new kitchen and new bathroom plus general painting and decorating. If house prices in the street are £100,000 and the house is on the market for £95,000 by the time I put in a new kitchen and bathroom I wouldn't make any profit on the property.

I recently purchased a property for £77,000 which came with a separate garage on the other side of the road. Garages were selling for around £6,000 and this one could be quickly sold. Houses in the street were selling for £110,000 to £115,000. I could see a quick capital gain between £33,000 and £44,000.

When I looked at this property I was amazed at how little work I needed to do to get the benefit of the capital gain. The previous owners had started to renovate the property but go into financial difficulty and had to sell. They had started to put in a new kitchen. All the cupboards and fittings were in place it just needed finishing and the flooring needed doing. The lounge and dining rooms were already decorated but there were no doors or door frames. The upstairs was in the same condition. A new bathroom had been started but not finished. A couple of windows needed replacing as the double glazing seals were broken. It looked much worse than it actually was.

I am lucky that my husband and I can do the repair work ourselves. So, we tiled the kitchen floor, refitted and finished the cupboards. Made up the door frames, skirting boards and bought new doors. Replaced the leaky windows, refitted the bathroom suite and carpeted the whole house. Total cost of refurbishment £1500. Time taken to complete the refurbishment was approximately three weeks. The property was then revalued and the house was valued at £115,000 and the garage at £8,000. A capital gain of £46,000 less £1500 for refurbishments, a net gain was achieved of £44,500 for three weeks work.

4. Good Opportunity for Capital Growth

For some reason most people are scared of capital growth. They imagine having to pay tax to the government and that this wipes out their profit. If I was going to sell the property I would probably have similar concerns but my system relies on good capital growth, holding on to the property and finding a tenant.

Using the property mentioned above in section 3, I will give an example of how my system works.

I purchased the property for £77,000. I obtained a buy-to-let mortgage for 85% of the purchase price, £65450 and put down a deposit of £11550. When the property was revalued the total value of the property was £115,000 and £8,000 for the garage which equals £123,000. I then remortgaged the property using another buy-to-let mortgage for 85% of the new value. This time the mortgage was for £104,550. The existing mortgage was repaid and I was left with cash in my hand of £39,100. This money is then mine to with as I choose as long as it is legal. There is no tax to pay on this money. (The Chancellor hasn't yet come up with a way of taxing loan money but I'm sure he's working on it!) I had enough money to put a deposit on two more properties plus pay myself an income for the three weeks work on the property. There is no capital gains tax to pay because I still own the property. And now I have a tenant in the property paying rent which covers the cost of the mortgage repayments. Plus that property has just provided me with the deposits to purchase another two properties.

5.   Good Rental Opportunities

When looking for a property I like to be sure I will get good rentals for it. So, I tend to look at the area. I am looking for properties which are modern. Most of my houses are less than forty years old. I find the more modern type houses rent much better than the older style houses. But that is only my opinion with the area I work in. It might be the reverse in another region. The house needs to be in a fairly good location. I am looking for areas where the properties are mainly owner/occupied. These areas are generally better maintained, gardens look better and the overall impression can add a few more thousand pounds to the property when it has been refurbished and revalued. The other criteria I am looking for is local amenities. That is how close is the school, the bus stop, the shopping centre or the local store. All these things make the property more attractive to rent and I can ask higher rents for them.

6. Finances Stack Up

By finances stack up I am talking about the costs for maintaining the property, compliances and mortgage repayments. The property also needs to provide me with a reasonable return.

In today's market with cheaper finance it is easier to balance the budget but what happens when mortgage rates go up which inevitably they will do. It might be five or ten years before they go up but you need to ensure you can weather any increases in the cost of finance.

If I borrow £100,000 at 3.99% then monthly repayments based on interest only will be £332.50 if interest rates go up to 5% repayments will be £416.66. Rents in my area for 3 bedroom house are circa £550. If interest rates are 5% I would have monthly net income of £550 - £416.66 = £133.34 per month. From this I have to pay insurance, roughly £10 per month, and gas compliances of £40 per year of £3.33. My profit is about £120 a month. If mortgages go above 5% I would still have a reasonable margin to be able to absorb the increase without getting into financial difficulty.

I have property in another region where rents are only £325 a month for a 3 bedroom house. As you can see the figures do not add up and the purchase is not viable. If I purchased a property in this region with a £100,000 mortgage I would be losing money every month and would quickly become bankrupt. Our aim is to make money not lose it.

Paperback version

http://www.amazon.co.uk/Make-Living-Property-Karen-Newton/dp/1480022195

Digital version

http://www.amazon.co.uk/Make-Living-From-Property-ebook/dp/B00AUJ79GY

Beginners Guide To The Sharemarket (Bonus Chapter)

Beginners Guide
To
Investing In The Sharemarket

REVISED EDITION

Karen Newton

Dollar Cost Averaging

When I lived overseas there was an expression called 'Dollar Cost Averaging'. It is one of the principals that I apply to buying shares. Simply put it means that I have a set amount of money each month that I use to buy shares. I buy at approximately the same time each month. Sometimes the price of the share is higher and sometimes it is lower. Over a period of time I work out the average price of the share. If I decide to sell then I will be in profit if I sell above the average price.

In the chart below I have invested one hundred pounds each month. The share price is fluctuating but I have worked out the average cost per share. For the example below I have not included tax or brokerage. If you are doing a similar exercise you should include tax and brokerage as they can have a big impact on the cost of your shares if you are dealing with small sums of money.

ABC Company

Purchasing £100 in shares each month

Date	Share Price	Share Bought	Total Shares Held	Average Cost per Share
January	50p	200	200	50p
February	53p	188	388	51.5p
March	45p	222	610	0.49p
April	47p	212	822	0.48p

As you can see from the above chart, over four months I have invested four hundred pounds and bought 822 shares. The average cost of the share is 48p. If I were to sell the shares at 49p I would make a profit. But without the chart I might be thinking that I was losing money because I remember paying 50p and 53p per share.

Now if I were to include a dividend in the equation you would be able to see the average cost of the share reduce in price.

Date	Share Price	Share Bought	Total Shares Held	Average Cost per Share
January	50p	200	200	50p
February	53p	188	388	51.5p
March	45p	222	610	0.49p
April	47p	212	822	0.48p
May (Dividend of £10 received and reinvested in shares	47p	21	843	0.47p

From this example you can see that the average cost of the share has reduced to 47p. I haven't spent any more money just reinvested the dividend. I could sell these shares for 48p and make a profit. Keeping records is important so you can monitor a buy and sell price of the share.

Paperback version

http://www.amazon.co.uk/Beginners-Guide-Investing-Sharemarket-Discover/dp/1482590921

Digital version

http://www.amazon.co.uk/Beginners-Guide-Investing-Sharemarket-ebook/dp/B00BI4SZ6I

Other Books By Karen Newton

29 Hours A Day

Have you ever wondered why some people seem to achieve so much during the day while you struggle with your workload.

29 hours a day shows you simple techniques to improve your time management skills and achieve more in a day than you thought possible.

Insider Guide to Investing in Art

Rembrandt, Monet and Picasso are some of the world's best know artists. Today their paintings are worth millions. Yet, they started their careers with little or no money needing supporters to help them survive from day to day.

Insider Guide to Investing in Art will help you identify the artists of today who are likely to be the successes of tomorrow. Buy their art today and it could be worth millions tomorrow.

Surviving 2012

As the Euro is on the brink of collapse discover how to protect yourself from the fallout.

In her latest book, Karen explains the importance of financial education and how building your knowledge will help you survive 2012 and beyond whether or not the euro fails.

Discover how Karen built an investment portfolio in excess of £10 million by borrowing £300 on a credit card.

Paperback version

http://www.amazon.co.uk/Surviving-2012-Mrs-Karen-Newton/dp/1477659951

Digital version

http://www.amazon.co.uk/Surviving-2012-ebook/dp/B008B8WUDS

www.ingramcontent.com/pod-product-compliance
Lightning Source LLC
Chambersburg PA
CBHW051330170526
45166CB00002B/754